Let's Get Acquainted!

Have you ever heard of the C[...]
Seventh-day Adventists and w[...]

Maybe you know a Seventh-day Adventist. A next-door neighbour. An acquaintance at work. Perhaps your doctor, electrician, or car salesman is an Adventist. Or perhaps you even have an Adventist somewhere in your family.

Then again, maybe you've never personally known any Adventists, but you've wondered, perhaps, why they go to church on Saturday — a different day than most Christians do. Why do they feel that what they eat and wear is so important? Why do they avoid certain forms of entertainment?

If you've ever wondered who Seventh-day Adventists are and what they believe, we'd like to introduce ourselves. We would like you to know us better. And we would also like to get to know you better. So in the next few pages, *Let's Get Acquainted!*

Let's begin by asking the obvious question —

Who Are the Seventh-day Adventists, Anyway?

Part of the answer is in our name:

"Seventh-day" refers to our belief in the seventh-day Sabbath (the fourth of the Bible's Ten Commandments). More about this a little later.

"Adventists" refers to our belief that Jesus Christ will soon return in person to this earth.

spot oN brothers & sisters

Who are Seventh-day Adventists? We are —

- Christians who love Jesus Christ and strive to make Him the centre of all we believe and do.
- A church that is eager to share the truth about what God is really like — as seen in the life, character, and death of Jesus Christ.
- Evangelical Protestants who accept the Bible as our authority for what to believe and how to live.
- A Christian fellowship committed to sharing with others certain Bible truths that over the centuries have been largely lost sight of — or that have become mixed with errors.
- A community of Christians deeply interested in health — health of mind, body, and spirit.
- Not a private club for saints. If anything, we're a hospital for sinners. But we rejoice in Christ's pardon for sin and in His power to deliver us from it.
- A rapidly growing worldwide fellowship of over sixteen million that is adding new members at a rate approaching 2,000 each day.

Before we go any further, maybe we should mention a couple of things that you may have heard we believe, but which we definitely do not!

- We do not believe that only Seventh-day Adventists will be saved — or that we are the only church around that teaches Bible truth.
- We do not believe we can earn salvation by works (being good). We do not believe that we are saved by Sabbath keeping, clean living, or keeping the Ten Commandments —

but by trusting entirely in Jesus Christ as our only source of salvation.

How Seventh-day Adventists Began

Though we did not officially organise as a church — a denomination — until 1863, our roots go back at least to the early 1800s. As the nineteenth century began, a great wave of interest in the Bible swept over America. This interest focused especially on the Bible prophecies concerning the Second Advent — the return to this world — of Jesus Christ.

Between 1831 and 1844, William Miller, a Baptist preacher and former army captain in the War of 1812, launched the "great Second Advent awakening," which eventually spread throughout most of the Christian world. Based on his study of the prophecy of Daniel 8:14, Miller calculated that Jesus would return to earth on October 22, 1844. When Jesus did not appear, Miller's followers experienced what came to be called "the Great Disappointment."

Most of the thousands who had joined the "great Second Advent awakening" left it, in deep disillusionment. A few, however, went back to their Bibles to find why they had been disappointed. Soon they concluded that the October 22 date had indeed been correct, but that Miller had predicted the wrong event for that day. They became convinced that the Bible prophecy predicted not that Jesus would return to earth in 1844, but that He would begin at that time a special ministry in heaven for His followers. They still looked for Jesus to come soon, however, as do Seventh-day Adventists yet today.

From this small group who refused to give up after the Great Disappointment arose several leaders who built the foundation of what would become the Seventh-day Adventist Church. Standing out among these leaders were a young couple — James and Ellen White — and a retired sea captain named Joseph Bates.

This small nucleus of "Adventists" began to grow — mainly in the New England states of America, where Miller's movement had begun. Ellen White, a mere teenager at the time of the Great Disappointment, grew into a gifted author, speaker, and administrator, who would become and remain the trusted spiritual counsellor of the Adventist family for more than seventy years until her death in 1915. Early Adventists came to believe — as have Adventists ever since — that she enjoyed God's special guidance as she wrote her counsels to the growing body of believers.

In 1860, at Battle Creek, Michigan, the loosely knit congregations of Adventists chose the name Seventh-day Adventist and in 1863 formally organised a church body with a membership of 3,500 — all in North America. By 1900 our membership had spread around the world and stood at 75,000. By the mid-1960s it had swelled to more than 1.5 million. And today, as we find ourselves in the twenty-first century, we have become one of the fastest-growing churches, with a membership of more than sixteen million and growing at nearly 2,000 a day.

What Seventh-day Adventists Believe

We do not have a formal "creed," because we do not want to "freeze truth in its tracks" and stop searching our Bibles for new truth — or for a clearer understanding of "old" truth.

But we Adventists have developed a Statement of Fundamental Beliefs which sets forth our current understanding of basic Bible truth. In this section, we will summarise how we understand the major teachings included in our statement of beliefs. We don't have space here to give a full presentation of each subject, but the summaries that follow will cover the major points of each one.

The Trinity

We believe that God is the Creator and King of the universe. Three distinct persons make up the Godhead: the Father, the Son, and the Holy Spirit. Although the word Trinity, which Christians use to describe this three-person God, is not in the Bible, the fact that God indeed consists of three persons is clearly taught there.

The three persons of the Godhead share certain common characteristics that set them apart from all other beings in the universe. God is immortal, all-powerful, all-knowing, unchangeable, and able to be everywhere at once. He is the source of all

Deut. 6:4
Gen. 1:26; 3:22
Matt. 3:16, 17
Matt. 28:19
John 14:16, 17
2 Cor. 13:14
1 Tim. 6:15, 16
Ps. 139:7-12
1 John 3:20
Jer. 32:17
Mal. 3:6
John 1:1-3

love, life, and power. And though He constantly supervises His entire vast creation, He is a personal God who wants to be the close Friend of each person on earth.

Perfect unity exists in the Trinity. Their goals, plans, and opinions are identical. They never disagree. Their very thoughts are open to each other. Though the Father, Son, and Holy Spirit are three separate persons, they think, act, and feel as one. They actually are one God in three persons.

Perfect equality also exists in the Trinity. All three of its members are fully God. No one member is less divine than the others. The Father did not create the Son or the Holy Spirit — all three have existed together from eternity and have no beginning. The Holy Spirit is not simply God's power — a divine force. He is a fully equal member of the Godhead.

God is infinitely patient, fair, and truthful. But the quality with which His name is most synonymous is love.

How Everything Began

It may take real effort, but try to imagine a time when there was no evil, no trouble, no sin. The Bible takes us back to just such a time — a time long, long ago — and a place far, far away. A place called heaven.

In heaven is God's throne — the headquarters of the vast universe. Countless angels — brilliant, intelligent, sinless beings whom God has created — bask in the joy and love of His presence. The highest angel over them all is called Lucifer — "the shining one."

Ezek. 28:11-19
Isa. 14:12-14
Rev. 12:3, 4, 7-9
Gen. 1:1-3:24
Job 1:6-12
Heb. 11:3
John 1:1-3
Col. 1:13-17
Rom. 5:12
Exod. 20:11
Heb. 1:2
Ps. 33:6-9

At some point in the years of eternity past, the Bible says, Lucifer began to become increasingly proud of his appearance and abilities. He determined to move up in heaven's scheme of things and eventually coveted equality with Jesus Christ Himself. When God the Father made it clear to him that this would never be — could never be — Lucifer became enraged. Before long, actual warfare broke out in heaven. Lucifer, along with a third of heaven's angels, was ultimately banned from heaven.

Meanwhile, in six literal days, God had created the earth and its first human beings — Adam and his wife Eve. He created for them a beautiful garden home called Eden, but warned them not to eat the fruit of a certain tree in the middle of the Garden — for if they did, they would die.

One day, however, Eve wandered alone to the foot of the tree, where a wonderful talking serpent in its branches (Lucifer, now called Satan, in disguise) told her that God's prohibition was an unfair lie. Eve believed Satan and ate some of the forbidden fruit. Soon Adam followed suit. Like Satan, they had mistrusted God and insisted on their own way. Sin, which had poisoned heaven, had now spoiled our newly created world. The great war between Christ and Satan had now moved to planet Earth.

When sin invaded earth, God could no longer directly speak and fellowship with human beings in person. Sin brought a great separation between the Creator and the humans He had created.

But God's love for us was so great that He determined somehow to break through the barrier sin had made. So He opened up a line of communication to the human race by inspiring godly men to write out His messages. These messages, brought together from many writers, form a book known by almost all humanity and loved by all of God's true followers. The book, of course, is the Holy Bible.

2 Pet. 1:20, 21
2 Tim. 3:15-17
John 5:39
John 17:17
Ps. 119:9, 11
2 Pet. 1:19
1 Pet. 1:23
Ps. 119:105
Heb. 4:12
Prov. 30:5, 6
Jer. 15:16
1 Thess. 2:13

Seventh-day Adventism began as a direct result of prayerful Bible study. And the Bible has been our foundation ever since. We value the Bible above all because it shows us the love of God as revealed in the life and character of Jesus Christ. We also prize it because it makes plain the way of salvation from sin — faith in the blood of Jesus.

Adventists believe that the whole Bible — Old and New Testaments — is the written Word of God, the infallible revelation of His will. Though the Bible had many writers, it had only one Author — the Holy Spirit. We believe that the Holy Spirit inspired the minds of the Bible writers with His thoughts and messages, which they then wrote out in their own words.

The Bible alone is our authority and standard for what to believe and how to live. It clearly sets forth truth and identifies error. The central personality of the Bible is Jesus — the central theme of the Bible is His love, demonstrated most fully by His death for us on the cross of Calvary. Adventists seek daily to get better acquainted with God through personal study of the priceless Book He has written for the human race.

Salvation

Adventists usually refer to the continuing war which Satan began long ago in heaven as "the great controversy between Christ and Satan." Sin entered the universe when Lucifer inexplicably became self-centred instead of God-centred. Selfishness is the very essence of sin. And sin is deadly. It contains within it the seeds of self-destruction.

Gen. 3:1-24
Rom. 5:12
Rom. 6:23
Rom. 5:8
John 3:16
1 Cor. 15:22
Eph. 2:8, 9
John 1:12
Rev. 3:20
John 3:1-15
Gal. 2:16, 20
Phil. 2:12, 13

Incredibly, Adam and Eve — though enjoying daily personal fellowship with God — were persuaded by Satan to doubt God's fairness and love. They selfishly chose their own way rather than God's, and the floodgates of sin opened on our world. And sin always leads to death — eternal oblivion.

But God had already planned for just such an emergency. Jesus the Son would come to this earth and become humanity's Substitute. He would reap the result of sin by dying in our place. Men and women would then have another chance to live forever — as God had originally intended.

Jesus did die for us all — on a horrible cross, surrounded

by men and women driven to a frenzy of hate by Satan, the great enemy. But after a Sabbath rest in the tomb, Jesus rose again, forever breaking the power of death for us.

When we accept Christ's life and death in our place, He justifies us — which means that He pardons us fully and accepts us as if we had never sinned. He also makes us new again (the new birth) and gives us power to live as He lived and love as He loved.

Adventists believe that salvation is only by God's grace through faith in Jesus as humanity's Substitute. We can add nothing to deserve or earn salvation; it is God's free gift. Everyone who in faith accepts Jesus as Saviour can rejoice in the full assurance of complete forgiveness and salvation.

We believe too that born-again Christians will give evidence in their lives of this great change. They will daily surrender themselves to the Lord Jesus and allow Him to bring about growth in grace and victory over sin.

Sabbath And The Family

Adventists believe that the Bible record of Creation is true — that God made the world in six literal days and rested on the seventh. And we rejoice in two magnificent gifts He gave to the human race at the end of Creation week. The first gift came when God performed the first wedding ceremony shortly after creating Adam and Eve on the sixth day. The gift of marital and family relationships God gave to humanity in Eden has brought great happiness to those who have invited Him

Exod. 20:3-17
John 14:15
Ps. 111:7, 8
Rev. 1:10
Mark 2:27, 28
Gen. 2:1-3
Ezek. 20:12, 20
Luke 4:16
Acts 18:1-4, 11
Isa. 58:13, 14
Eph. 5:22-28

to be the Lord of their homes and families. God gave His second great gift to our original parents the very next day. The Bible says that on the seventh day of Creation week God rested, not because He was tired, but because He had finished His work. God then set apart the seventh day as a special holy day. The very word Sabbath means "rest." Later, in the fourth of the Bible's Ten Commandments, God asked His followers to "Remember the sabbath day, to keep it holy." Exodus 20:8.

Still later, Christ came to earth to show us God's love and to save us. On Calvary's cross that dark Friday afternoon He proclaimed, "It is finished!" Then He rested over the sacred hours of the Sabbath.

To us today, the Bible makes it plain that the Sabbath is a memorial of God's power as Creator — but also of His power as our Re-creator. The Sabbath is also a celebration of God's power to deliver us from the power of sin.

But above all, the Sabbath is a constant invitation to rest from our works as Jesus did from His. Resting in Christ's finished work for us, we are delivered from trying to earn salvation by our own works — by being good. How sad that some actually see Sabbath keeping as legalistic — a symbol of salvation by works — when each week the Sabbath points us away from human works to rest in God's creative, saving work for us.

Though the rebellion against God which Satan exported from heaven to earth soon enlisted the majority of the human race, there have always been those who responded to God's appeal to follow Him.

Acts 7:38
Eph. 2:19, 20
Heb. 10:23-25
Matt. 16:13-24
Matt. 28:19, 20
Rom. 12:4, 5
1 Cor. 12:12-27
Eph. 4:4-16
Rev. 12:17
Rev. 14:6-12
Rev. 18:1-4
Rev. 19:10

In earth's earliest history, the families of faithful patriarchs composed His "church." Later, God chose the nation of Israel to be His "church" — to represent Him to the world. And before He left earth to return to heaven, Christ launched the New Testament church, which He described as His body.

Christ's church today is a spiritual body made up of all who accept Him as their Saviour and Lord. Though many denominations exist, Adventists believe that Christ's true followers — His body — may be found scattered among all these organisations.

Salvation does not come through joining any church organisation. Salvation comes through trusting in the Head of the church — Jesus Christ. But those who truly trust in Christ will quite naturally want to become a part of His church — the body of Christ on earth. It is really not possible to accept fully the Head of the church while rejecting fellowship with His body.

The purpose of the church is to provide for group worship of God, for the mutual encouragement and fellowship of its members, and for reaching out to the world with the good news about Christ and His salvation.

Although we as Adventists do not see ourselves as better

than any other true Christians, we do believe that — in fulfilment of Bible prophecy — God has called Adventists into existence just before the second coming of Christ to help restore certain Bible truths that have long been lost sight of. We believe that God has asked us to proclaim a special message to the world and to other Christians, which will produce a faithful remnant of the church to meet Christ when He comes.

Baptism And The Lord's Supper

Baptism is an outward symbol of a profound inner change. Baptism symbolises the death and burial of our old life of sin and selfishness and our resurrection to a whole new life of dependence on Christ. According to the Bible, we become a part of the body of Christ (His church) by baptism.

Rom. 6:3, 4
1 Cor. 12:12, 13
Matt. 3:13-16
Matt. 28:19, 20
Mark 16:15, 16
Col 2:12
Gal. 3:27
Acts 2:38
Acts 8:36-39
John 13:1-7
Matt. 26:26-30
1 Cor. 11:23-30

We Seventh-day Adventists follow the example of Christ's own baptism — baptism by immersion — that is, by being lowered completely beneath the water. Baptism as a symbol of death, burial, and resurrection loses its significance, we feel, when Christians are baptised simply by pouring or sprinkling. And since baptism signifies a personal decision to accept Jesus as Saviour, we do not baptise infants.

A second spiritual ordinance, or ceremony, observed by Seventh-day Adventists is the Lord's Supper. Just before His crucifixion, Christ met with His disciples in an upper room somewhere in Jerusalem and instituted a special memorial of His death for us all. He shared with them unleavened bread as a symbol of His body — soon to be sacrificed on the cross — and grape juice as a symbol of the blood He would soon shed. Then He asked them to observe this special memorial in the future, until His second coming.

Just prior to that first Lord's Supper, Christ instituted another spiritual ceremony. As an example of humility, service, and spiritual cleansing, Christ washed the feet of His disciples and asked His followers to do as He had done.

Jesus did not say how often the Lord's Supper or the footwashing service should be observed. Adventists usually celebrate them quarterly — every three months. Men and women meet separately to wash each other's feet, then meet together to celebrate the Lord's Supper. Adventists practise what is called an "open Communion," meaning that Christians of any denomination are invited to join them in the observance of these special memorials Jesus gave.

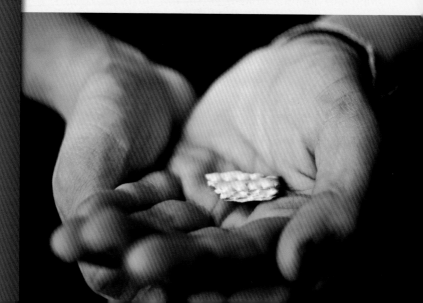

Through the Holy Spirit, God gives special spiritual gifts to each true Christian. God intends that, just as each part of a human body fulfils a specific function, each member of His spiritual body will also fulfil a specific function through exercising the spiritual gifts He has given.

Eph. 4:4-16
1 Cor. 12:1-11
Rom. 12:4-8
1 Pet. 4:10, 11
1 Cor. 1:4-7
Joel 2:28, 29
Rev. 12:17
Rev. 19:10
Amos 3:7
2 Chron. 20:20
Jer. 28:9
1 John 4:1-3, 6

The Holy Spirit chooses what spiritual gifts each Christian receives. Some of these gifts are most useful for building up the body of Christ — that is, for ministering to those already in the church. Others are designed primarily for reaching out to win others to Christ and His church. If each member fully exercises his or her gifts, the church will be growing and vigorous. Some spiritual gifts mentioned in the Bible include wisdom, faith, healing, miracles, prophecy, evangelism, teaching, and pastoring.

One of the gifts which the Bible says will be present in the church just before Christ's second coming is the gift of prophecy. This gift often includes a special ability to publicly expound the Scriptures. But it also may include the ability to predict future events and to deliver special messages from God to His people.

Seventh-day Adventists believe that the gift of prophecy in all its fullness was evident in the life and work of one of its founding pioneers — Mrs. Ellen G. White. Through scores of books and magazine articles, as well as through public speaking, Ellen White faithfully shared God's messages to our young and growing church.

Though Adventists do not believe that Mrs. White's writings in any way take the place of the Bible or add to it, we are convinced that she enjoyed God's special guidance and inspiration as she wrote. Her books such as *Steps to Christ* and *The Desire of Ages* have led thousands to see the character of Jesus more clearly.

Christian Lifestyle

When we turn our backs on self and the world to follow Jesus, the Bible says we become altogether new in Him. We no longer enjoy what the world enjoys. We experience a radical change in our thoughts, desires, and behaviour. This change extends to every area of life. Seventh-day Adventists have found that the Bible has much to say in describing how true Christians live. Because the Bible teaches that the human body is the temple of the Holy Spirit, Adventists strive to avoid anything that would weaken or endanger their bodies. Thus we steer clear of alcohol, tobacco in all its forms, recreational drugs, and caffeinated beverages. We also avoid using the flesh of animals which the Bible identifies as unclean. In fact, many Adventists have adopted a vegetarian diet as most conducive to excellent health. The Adventist commitment to health may also be seen in our many hospitals and clinics, in our stop-smoking and weight-loss programmes, and in our community cooking schools.

We also believe that the Bible teaches that Christians

2 Cor. 6:14-18
1 John 2:15-17
2 Cor. 5:17
1 Cor. 3:16, 17
1 Cor. 6:19, 20
Lev. 11:1-47
Rom. 8:5
Phil 4:8
1 Pet. 3:3, 4
1 Tim. 2:9, 10
Matt. 3:8-12
Lev. 27:30, 32

should concentrate more on beautifying their characters than on decorating their bodies. Therefore we believe in dressing modestly and simply, relying not on jewellery and ornaments, but on good health, for a winsome appearance.

Because the Bible counsels Christians to guard their thoughts and to live exemplary lives, we Adventists are careful in what we view and do in our leisure time. We avoid those forms of entertainment that would undermine our relationship to Christ.

Finally, Adventists believe that true conversion reaches even to our possessions. We believe in tithing our income for the support of God's ministry — and in giving generous offerings to advance God's work in the world.

Exod. 25:8
Exod. 29:38, 39
Heb. 8:1-13
Heb. 9:1-28
Heb. 10:9-14
Dan. 7:9, 10
Dan. 8:14
Dan. 9:24-27
Rev. 14:6, 7
Rev. 22:11, 12
Lev. 16:1-34
Lev. 23:26-28

The Sanctuary

In both the Old and New Testaments, the sanctuary is the name given to the place where God lives. God asked His Old Testament church in the wilderness — the people of Israel — to actually build a literal sanctuary. He gave them the plans for it patterned after the sanctuary in heaven where His throne is. This Old Testament sanctuary — and the temple that later succeeded it — illustrated how God saves us and deals with the problem of sin. In its architecture, sacrifices, and services, it pointed to Christ's work as our Saviour.

The priests of the Old Testament sanctuary carried forward their work on Israel's behalf each day in the first

room — called the Holy Place. But once a year, on the Day of Atonement, the high priest entered the second room of the sanctuary — the Most Holy Place — carrying the blood of a goat with which he symbolically cleansed the sanctuary of its accumulation of sins. This represented the work Jesus would do in reality.

On the basis of Bible prophecies in Daniel 8 and 9, Seventh-day Adventists believe that in the year 1844 Christ entered the Most Holy Place of the real sanctuary in heaven and began there a special "Day of Atonement" ministry for us. This work is going on now and will continue until shortly before His second coming.

Because Satan accuses Christ's followers of being great sinners who shouldn't be saved, Christ — before the whole universe — must defend not only His followers, but His right to save them. As both our Sacrifice and our High Priest, He is able to point out that the sins of His followers are covered by His blood — that they are to be saved not because of their goodness, but His.

Understanding the lessons of the heavenly sanctuary is by

no means impossible, but it does require earnest study — particularly of Bible prophecy. In this brief description, we can only touch the surface of this great truth — a truth which provides unparalleled views of Christ's work and character.

What Happens To Us When We Die?

What happens to us when we die? Do we ever live again? Do we go to heaven or to hell as soon as we die?

Fortunately, the Bible gives us clear answers to these questions. According to God's Word, we human beings do not have souls — we are souls. At creation, God breathed the gift of life into the body He had formed for Adam, and Adam became a living soul, or person. At death, the gift of life returns to God who gave it, and our bodies return to the dust from which God first made them. But the gift of life that returns to God at death is not a conscious "soul," fully aware of what is happening around it. The Bible says that death is a time of unconscious oblivion — that the dead are totally unaware of what is taking place around them. The Bible also makes it clear that at death we do not go directly to heaven or to hell, but to the grave — there to remain until resurrected later by Christ. Most of the world and many Christians today believe that human beings are immortal — that though our bodies may die, our "souls" live forever. But the Bible teaches otherwise. It clearly states that human beings are mortal and that only God is immortal. But it does say that, at the second coming

Gen. 2:7
Eccl. 12:7
Ps. 104:29
John 11:11-14
Eccl. 9:5, 6
Ps. 146:3, 4
Ps. 6:5
Ps. 115:17
Job 7:9, 10
Job 14:12
1 Tim. 6:15, 16
1 Cor. 15:51-55

of Christ, He will give the gift of immortality to all His true followers. When Jesus was here on earth, His preferred term for death was *sleep*. Sleep usually implies waking up again. And since, in God's reckoning, we were all included in Christ as our representative Man when He rose from the dead, He has broken the power of death for all of us. Some of us may "sleep" for a while before Christ returns, but death has been defeated, and, if we belong to Christ, we will awaken again someday.

The Second Advent Of Christ

One of the clearest teachings and most glorious promises of all the Bible is that Jesus Christ will soon return in person to this earth. As the Adventist half of our denominational name indicates, we eagerly look forward to the return of our Saviour, King, and best Friend.

Acts 1:9-11
John 14:1-3
Matt. 24:14
Ps. 50:3
Rev. 1:7
Matt. 16:27
1 Thess. 4:13-18
1 Cor. 15:51-55
Rev. 20:1-10
Rev. 21:1-22:5
Matt. 24:42-44
Titus 2:11-13

When Jesus left this earth not long after His resurrection, He promised to return again and take His followers to be with Him. Earlier, He had provided several key signs that would indicate when His return was drawing near. One of the chief signs, rapidly being fulfilled today, was the preaching of the gospel — the good news about Jesus — to the whole world.

The Bible says that Jesus will not return secretly, but that everyone on earth will see and hear His coming. He will arrive in kingly glory on a great cloud, with all His angels. He will call to life again His followers who have fallen asleep in death. Then His followers who are alive when He returns will be caught up with the resurrected ones into the great cloud to be with Him. The wicked of all ages who sleep in death will sleep on when Jesus comes. And the wicked who are alive to see Him return will be destroyed by the intense glory of their rejected Saviour.

The Bible says that Christ will return to heaven with His followers, for 1,000 years (sometimes called the millennium). During this time the earth lies desolate and unpopulated except by Satan and his angels. At the end of the 1,000 years, Christ and His followers will return to this earth, and the holy city, New Jerusalem, will come down from heaven. The wicked of all ages will be resurrected to see Christ return. The wicked, led by Satan and his fallen angels, are about to storm the New Jerusalem to take it by force, when they will be destroyed by a fire that cleanses the earth of every trace of sin. This is the true hell of the Bible.

Then God will create the earth anew, and this new earth will become the joyous, sinless home of Christ's redeemed for all eternity. The great controversy will be ended — and peace will reign forever.

How the Seventh-day Adventist Church Is Organised

The Seventh-day Adventist Church has from its beginning chosen a representative form of government. The key unit of its organisation is the local congregation.

The congregations in a given geographical area make up a local conference or mission. Within the United Kingdom we have two conferences (North England and South England) and three missions (Irish, Scottish and Welsh).

The local conference/mission appoints ministers for individual congregations. Adventist ministers are all paid from the tithes sent to the local conference by the members of its individual congregations — and all the ministers receive the same salary, adjusted for regional costs of living, whether their congregation is large or small.

A number of local conferences and/or missions together form a union conference. The entire world is divided into thirteen divisions — each composed of several union conferences. Together, these divisions make up the worldwide level of church government called the General Conference.

The world headquarters of the Seventh-day Adventist Church — its General Conference — is located in Silver Spring, Maryland, USA. The chief executive of the church is its president, who is elected (or reelected) every five years at a General Conference session. Delegates from each level of church government convene for this quinquennial session to hear reports and transact business that relates to the world church.

Primary Activities of the Seventh-day Adventist Church

Adventists are busy, active, involved Christians. This activity takes many forms — chief among them the following:

Worship — Most congregations begin their Sabbath (Saturday) services at 9:30 A.M. with Sabbath School (similar to the Sunday Schools of other denominations). Sabbath School members engage in group Bible study, outreach, and worship of God through music.

At about 11:00 A.M., the worship hour begins. The order of service is similar to that in most other Protestant churches and culminates with the preaching of the Word.

Most Adventist churches also hold a midweek prayer meeting (often on Wednesday evening), and many hold other meetings for youth, for children, and for those who wish to do community service work.

Evangelism — Winning others to Jesus Christ and His truth is the single greatest desire and effort of Seventh-day Adventists. Through public crusades, personal Bible studies, literature distribution, radio and television broadcasts, and other avenues, we reach out to our neighbours and friends to share the gospel of Jesus Christ.

Education — Adventists believe firmly in the clear advantages of Christian education. We operate nearly 6,000 schools worldwide — from elementary level through college and university. In an age when so much of public education seems to be adopting the philosophy of secular humanism, we believe that it is vital to provide students with an education that upholds the spiritual dimension.

Health And Medical — Because we Adventists are interested in the whole person — the physical as well as the spiritual — we place great emphasis on health. Over 500 Adventist hospitals, sanitariums, clinics, and dispensaries are scattered around the globe. The Adventist Church offers stop-smoking and weight-loss classes, vegetarian cooking schools, and stress-reduction programmes to the general public. Our medical school, hospital, and research centre at Loma Linda University in southern California are at the forefront of research and innovation in health and medicine.

Disaster And Famine Relief — Through the efforts of the Adventist Development and Relief Agency (ADRA), our church is able to respond quickly to disasters anywhere in the world with food, clothing, and medical supplies. In addition, ADRA carries on a continuous programme of famine relief in drought-stricken areas of the world.

Community Services — Many local Seventh-day Adventist churches operate Community Service Centres, staffed with church volunteers who assist the needy and homeless in their communities. Most of these centres keep in stock clothing, bedding, and a limited supply of canned food for those most in need.

Publishing — With nearly 60 publishing houses around the world, Seventh-day Adventists are totally committed to sharing God's good news with the world through the printed page. Each year, scores of periodicals, hundreds of books, and thousands of small tracts are published and sold or given away worldwide. In the United States, the church operates two large publishing houses — in the UK, The

Stanborough Press Ltd., the Seventh-day Adventist publishing house for the United Kingdom and the Republic of Ireland, is based in Grantham, Lincolnshire.

Adventist Book Centres offer a large selection of books, music, magazines, study curriculum materials, and sharing tools. All these materials are also available for purchase on the Internet at www.AdventistBookCenter.com.

Communication — Adventists were among the first to bring the gospel of Jesus Christ to both radio and television. The Voice of Prophecy radio broadcast began in 1930 with H. M. S. Richards as its founding speaker/director. That responsibility is carried forward today by Pastor Fred Kinsey.

Faith For Today, the oldest denominationally sponsored religious broadcast on television, first aired in 1950, with William A. Fagal as speaker/director. Later developments of this ministry have included Faith For Today's popular "Lifestyle Magazine," hosted by Dan Matthews, and "The Evidence," hosted by Pastor Dwight Nelson.

The It Is Written telecast, with George E. Vandeman as speaker/director, began in 1955. Mark Finley later succeeded Pastor Vandeman as speaker/director, and the telecast continues to apply Bible counsel to contemporary issues and human needs.

In 1974 Breath of Life, a national television broadcast, began reaching out to the black population of North America with C. D. Brooks as speaker/director. Walter Pearson is now the speaker/director of the telecast.

All of these broadcasts are produced by the Adventist Media Centre in Simi Valley, California.

Questions About Seventh-day Adventists

Occasionally, people confuse us with other religious groups. Or they hear things about us that are inaccurate. Earlier in this booklet, we addressed two such misconceptions: that Adventists believe we alone will be saved and that we believe in salvation through our good works (legalism).

Now we'd like to answer a few more of the questions people sometimes ask us.

Q. *Are you the church that does not believe in blood transfusions?*
A. No. You may be confusing us with the Jehovah's Witnesses.

Q. *Don't you have a lot of churches in Utah?*
A. We do have a number of churches in the state of Utah. But you may be confusing us with the Church of Jesus Christ of Latter-day Saints (Mormons), headquartered in Salt Lake City.

Q. *Aren't Seventh-day Adventists a cult?*
A. Most cults can be identified by their nonbiblical doctrines as well as by their use of psychological coercion in attempting to control the thinking and behaviour of their adherents. Many cults also deny the deity of Jesus Christ. We Adventists base all our doctrines firmly upon the Bible, and we believe fervently in the divinity of Jesus. We reject as incompatible with true Christianity any form of force or pressure in gaining or retaining converts.

Q. *Do Adventists speak in tongues?*

A. As noted in the section on what we believe, we most certainly believe in the gifts of the Spirit, including the gift of tongues. However, we believe that when Paul discusses this gift in 1 Corinthians 14, his clear emphasis is on the communication of an intelligible message. He speaks against the use of a meaningless gibberish. We believe that the gift of tongues at Pentecost gave the disciples a miraculous ability to speak languages they had never learned before so that they could witness to those from other countries who were visiting Jerusalem.

Q. *Do Adventists have women pastors?*

A. A few women currently serve as Adventist pastors, though the church has not yet ordained any women to the gospel ministry.

Q. *Hasn't the Adventist Church a number of times set a date for the second coming of Christ?*

A. Though William Miller's movement (see the section on how Adventists began) did set a time for the return of Christ — and while it is true that some who joined Miller in looking for Christ to return in the year 1844 later helped establish the Seventh-day Adventist Church — the church itself has never set a date for the Second Coming. We hold to the Bible teaching that no one can know the exact date of Christ's return. (See Mark 13:32.)

We probably haven't answered all your questions. For more information about Seventh-day Adventists — who we

are and what we believe — you may find the following
Internet sources and telephone numbers helpful. Or tick one
of the requests on the next page.

British Union Conference of Seventh-day Adventists,
www.adventist.org.uk • 01923 672251
General Conference of Seventh-day Adventists, the church's
world headquarters. *www.adventist.org*
Hope Channel, the TV channel of the Seventh-day Adventist
Church in the United Kingdom. *www.hopetv.org.uk*
Adventist Book Centres, browse or order church publications
online: *www.AdventistBookCenter.com* • 01476 539900
The Stanborough Press Ltd., the church's publishing house in
the United Kingdom and Ireland. *www.stanboroughpress.co.uk*
Adventist Review, the official publication of the world church.
www.adventistreview.org
Breath of Life, a television outreach ministry of the Seventh-
day Adventist Church. *http://www.breathoflife.tv/index.php*
Ellen G. White Estate, custodian of Ellen White's written
materials. *www.whiteestate.org*
Faith For Today, a television outreach ministry of the
Seventh-day Adventist Church. *www.faithfortoday.tv*
It Is Written, a television outreach ministry of the Seventh-
day Adventist Church. *www.iiw.org*
Seventh-day Adventist Theological Seminary, Andrews
University, Berrien Springs, MI, USA. *www.andrews.edu/SEM/*
Seventh-day Adventist College of Higher Education, Newbold
College, Berkshire, England. *www.newbold.ac.uk*
Voice of Prophecy, a radio outreach ministry of the Seventh-
day Adventist Church. *www.vop.com*

Where Can I Learn More About Seventh-day Adventists?

☐ Send me a free copy of Focus, a magazine of spiritual life.

☐ Enrol me in one of your free Bible courses.

☐ I want information about your stop-smoking plan.

☐ I would like more information about the Bible prophecies of Daniel and Revelation.

☐ Send me the address of the nearest Adventist Church.

☐ I would like to know more about Seventh-day Adventists and what they believe.

Name _____

Address _____

_____

Postcode _____

Telephone (optional)_____

email (optional) _____

Complete this coupon and mail to:
Adventist Discovery Centre
Stanborough Park
Watford
WD25 9JU

For a faster service telephone 01923 672606 or Fax 01923 894835 or visit our website: *www.discoveronline.org.uk*

pass it on

The Adventist Discovery Centre –
Where hope comes to life, and life takes on new meaning.

Something
WONDERFUL

FOR YOU

FREE Bible Guides that make a difference to your life.

Find your purpose
• Where are you headed? • Where is the world headed? • Explore the meaning of your life. **DISCOVER** how the Bible can make a difference in your life.

www.discoveronline.org.uk

Adventist Discovery Centre, Stanborough Park, Watford, WD25 9JU.

A NEW UNDERSTANDING OF THE BIBLE
RELIEVES TENSION AND ANXIETY,
PROMOTES HEALTH AND LONG LIFE.

SEVENTH-DAY
ADVENTIST
CHURCH